ENDORSEMENTS

"Dotty has a Christ-driven love for the precious Jewels in the strip clubs. To see the love of Jesus poured out on these women through Dotty is beautiful. She gives of herself to these Jewels not only inside the club, but she has met with some of them outside the club at their request. There is a bond between Dotty and these women that can only come from the Lord. I am grateful to the Lord for giving me the opportunity to bring Jesus into the club with Dotty, who has been anointed for this work. I am so glad that this book is now available for people to see the heart of the Lord toward those who have been hurting and abused."

— Shelley Albert, Minnesota

"This book is a wonderful testimony of how the Holy Spirit works through Dotty, her husband Jon, and others (team Jesus). She goes into places with the armor of God that most of us would fear to tread! This inspirational book will bless your heart! You will get to know the sacrifices that Dotty has made to deliver the cross to people that normally would not hear the Gospel. She is a firecracker in God's Army!"

— Pastor Johnnie and Janna Armes, Church of the Revelation, Jonesboro, Indiana

Jesus in the Strip Clubs

FINDING HIDDEN JEWELS IN THE NIGHT

Dotty Zens

EDITED BY JON ZENS

Copyright © 2023 by Dotty Zens, First Edition

Scriptures taken from the Holy Bible, New International Version®, NIV®. Copyright © 1973, 1978, 1984, 2011 by Biblica, Inc.™ Used by permission of Zondervan. All rights reserved worldwide. www.zondervan.com The "NIV" and "New International Version" are trademarks registered in the United States Patent and Trademark Office by Biblica, Inc.™

Scripture taken from the Contemporary English Version © 1991, 1992, 1995 by American Bible Society. Used by Permission.

Cover Painting by Dotty Zens
Cover Design by Rafael Polendo (polendo.net)
Interior Layout by Matthew J. Distefano

ISBN PRINT 978-1-957007-61-8
This volume is printed on acid free paper and meets ANSI Z39.48 standards.
Printed in the United States of America

Published by Quoir
Chico, California
www.quoir.com

CONTENTS

ORIENTATION

Since Dotty's narrative is not written in chronological order, we thought it would be helpful to the readers to give a brief overview of her journey into the strip club ministry. In this way, the pieces will hopefully fit together as her story unfolds.

When we were in New Zealand in 1994, a brother had mentioned to us a ministry in Manila/Quezon City, Philippines, that helped women out of prostitution. So, in late 2003 we began to plan a trip to the Philippines during which we would visit groups that functioned outside the institutional churches. Once we were there in early 2004, we contacted that ministry and ended up spending time with their street ministry workers both at the beginning and end of our trip. in early 2004. While we were there, they told us about an anti-prostitution conference that was to take place in May, 2004, in Green Lake, Wisconsin, only five hours east of us!

We attended this electrifying gathering, along with about 250 other people from all over the world. The emerging grassroots organization was called ICAP, International Christian Alliance on Prostitution. We also attended ICAP conferences held at Green Lake in 2006 and 2008. In 2009 we went to the ICAP meeting in Manila, Philippines, where Dan Allender was the keynote speaker. Dotty made a total of four trips to the Philippines, and during one trip she worked with a ministry that went into strip bars in Angeles City.

The next ICAP conference was in Green Lake in 2011. A turning point happened for Dotty at this gathering—she met Renee Wurzer, who was part of a strip club ministry near Eau Claire, Wisconsin, called Whispered Hopes. For a year and a half, Dotty drove an hour and a half each way to be mentored by Rene in several clubs. After that training period, Renee encouraged Dotty to start visiting clubs nearer to us.

During the Christmas season in 2012, Dotty and Heather visited Club #1, the club that is closest to where we live. Then, on Thanksgiving, 2013, Dotty and Brianna had their first visit to Club #2, which was a two and a half hour drive from us.

Other women have gone into clubs with Dotty over the years: Heather, Brianna, Sue, Cheryl, Karlie, Carol, Melanie, BK, Angy and her mother, Katie Jean, Becky J., Jenni, Jennifer S., Missy, Carol, Karrie, Heidi, Jennifer, Shelley, Becky H., Bonnie and possibly others.

As of December, 2022, Dotty is still going into Clubs #1 and #2. In addition, she has also visited clubs during our travels to Cancun; Jacksonville, FL; Tampa, FL; Melbourne, FL; Brunswick, GA; Stanley, WI; Elk River, WI; and Milwaukee, WI.

— JZ

DEDICATION AND THANKS

To my husband, Jon Zens. There are not many husbands who would patiently wait in a car in a strip club parking lot while his wife ministers to the women inside for typically two hours. He prays and he visits via phone with brethren while I'm in the club. He *is* patient! He knows God is at work inside. It later occurred to me that he is a testimony outside the club, as well as me being inside the club. I am very grateful. Also, my night vision is not very good, so I would not be able to go to the clubs if he did not drive me to them. When I am alone inside a club, he is with me on the outside. And I want to thank him for all the long, tedious hours he put into editing this manuscript.

To Renee Wurzer. She has been my mentor in the clubs, and her example has been beyond wonderful. Through her genuine sincerity, Renee has taught me that these Jewels are no different than the rest of us, and her love and respect for them has penetrated my innermost being.

To Cheryl Voyles. She has walked into the clubs side by side with me many times. Her sincere love for these precious Jewels and her gentleness has given me such respect for her. The significant healing Cheryl has experienced from her past trauma is a big part of why the club Jewels are drawn to her and embrace her hugs.

So thankful for those who invested their time into reading this manuscript and gave such helpful thoughts and edits: Shelley Albert, Marilyn Davis, Rebecca DeWane, Sue and Christa Heumann, Mary Ellen Robinson, Shari Rodriguez, Catherine Seebald (kudos), Renee Wurzer, and B K Zimmer.

1

OUR JERICHO

I had driven by that abandoned building a number of times, and it just looked so strange. And then sometimes Jon and I would drive by and there would be lights on. Now, if that isn't scary enough, there was a chain link fence about ten feet high with barbed wire at the top that went around the east side of the building. I just sensed that it was put there so that women could not escape, and that thought just absolutely terrified me. I did not know until much later that this was the strip club the Lord was calling me to go into.

Sometimes I had a hard time sleeping. One night I couldn't sleep, so I got up and sat in my prayer chair and prayed and wept. And then I opened my Bible. And what Scripture do you suppose the Lord led me to? The story of Jericho's walls collapsing. That huge, high stone wall was so thick that people lived inside its structure. How amazing is that? Why in the world should I be terrified, if what I was looking at was a chain link fence that I could see right through? If the Lord could knock down the stone walls of Jericho, then this puny chain link fence was nothing against the power of God.

A few days later, on December 20, 2012, my dear friend Heather and I knew God had chosen the two of us to go into this club together. If you live in the Midwest, you might understand -- several days later when we actually went to the club, there was an ice storm. The rest of my team that I had trained with at another club was a one and a half hours drive away, and had planned on piling into a car and joining us on opening night. Opening night is the evening you first enter a club and ask someone in charge for permission for you to come in, visit with the women and give them presents.

When Heather and I got to the club that night, she looked at me and said, "Do you think we are supposed to do a prayer walk around the walls of this building and pray concerning the evil spirits?" How amazing is this? Ever since I had opened to that passage about the Jericho wall, I felt strongly I was to do a prayer walk around that building, but I had not even mentioned it to my husband. So no one knew that's what I was thinking. When Heather asked me that, I said, *"Yes!"*

Then we trudged through the twelve inches of freshly dropped snow and marched around that building, circling seven times. I know in the original event they actually went around thirteen times, but we felt seven was ample. We got into the car when we were finished praying for the subduing of the evil spirits connected to the lies that the men and women believed.

When we got inside the car, Heather shut her door and said, "The walls are down!" Streams of tears were flowing down both our cheeks, tears of joy. The Lord had told me to bring along Communion for Heather and I. So we sat in the car and talked to Jesus and honored Him in the breaking of bread and the drinking of wine, symbolizing His authority by His resurrected body from the grave over all the spirits, which authority He has also given to us. Needless to say, it was a fantastic, sweet, sweet time!

2

SPREADING MY WINGS

I 'll never forget when my mentor, Renee, gently encouraged me to leave my comfortable nest. I was like a little bird who was so happy and content in it. So at home in the club we had gone to for a year and a half together. She had already been going to this club for several years. Renee kept telling me there was a club closer to me that needed ministry. Oh, yes. That's the Jericho club—the one with the big ten-foot fence around it. I was terrified to go into this club by myself without my mentor, although she said she would come when she could. Renee strongly encouraged me to start in this club before Christmas, 2012, which gave me three months. Although I put it off repeatedly, I knew the time was coming.

3

GIDEON'S ARMY

I had spent two weeks prior to this opening night gathering presents—remakes of thrift store treasures—and wrapping them beautifully. I have literally never made gifts look so attractive in my entire life. I had a large clear tote full of presents because I had no idea how many women would be in the club that night. For our opening night, Jon had looked up to see who the owner/manager was. It was "S," who was the bartender and manager for that evening.

Early that morning, when the team from an hour and a half away had planned on coming with us, we had an ice storm that wreaked havoc on the winding road from their place to this new club. It was touch and go all day long as to whether they'd be able to join us.

Just before it would have been time for them to leave their area to come join Heather and me, we got the fateful call: the roads were too icy and it was too windy to make it safely, and so they were not able to come. I had a gut feeling all morning that this would happen. So I asked Renee on the phone, "Are you comfortable with Heather and I going in alone?" She said, "Absolutely!" That was confirmation that the Lord was with Heather and me, and by His strength, we could do it together. That was all I needed to hear, so we packed up all of the treasures we had gathered, food to take to the women, and decorations for the little table.

Earlier that morning, when I was seeking the Lord about entering the club, the Lord gave me the story of Gideon. Now you remember Gideon had a large army, but he was coming up against a ginormous army. Nevertheless, the Lord wanted Gideon to know absolutely that the battle is not ours, it's the Lord's—it's His battle, and He wants all the glory that is due His holy name. So I wondered all day if my team would truly be able to join us, since Gideon's army was whittled down to a tiny little speck in the dust.

There was another scene in Gideon's story that caught my attention. Gideon was told by God to take a friend with him and hide behind a huge rock near where the enemy was resting before the big battle. So while Gideon and his friend hid behind the rock, they were able to hear two men talking. One said to the other, as I remember it, that he'd had a dream in which a huge loaf of bread came down from heaven and destroyed the entire army. The other man said, "Oh my goodness, I know what this is. This is a dream from God and we are going to be destroyed!"

So I had this in the back of my mind. As I entered this club with Heather, I saw the bartender and recognized her from the picture Jon had of her as the manager for the evening. Now I was already prejudiced against women who control other women, especially in sexual slavery. They seem to be hard-hearted and have worse ways of controlling the women than even some of the men. So already I did not like "S." (Initials will be used to protect the identity of some individuals). When I saw her, I knew she was the one I needed to ask for permission to visit with the women. She was leaning over the bar talking to a male customer, but I knew he wasn't really listening to her. He was there for other reasons, but as she was pouring out her story, I listened to her. I heard her say that she had been very sick, and I knew that man couldn't care less, but the Lord gave me love and compassion for her. So I pulled out of my bag a loaf of homemade bread I had taken out of the oven shortly before we came. Even though "S" had mentioned she had been throwing up the night before, she grabbed the loaf like it was a gold nugget. I was so tickled. So we asked her permission to visit with the women and give them presents, and she gave us consent.

We set up two tiny tables with bar stools around them, covered them with beautiful table cloths, and made them look very fancy, Then we set the food on one table and the presents on the other. It was an unbelievably joyful night, my first visit without my mentor and with my buddy, Heather. That was such a great time! The first young woman who came over to us was reticent. She could tell we were "church ladies," and most of the women I encounter have a very bad experiences with church ladies, religious women, who shake their fingers at them, telling them that they were doing "no-no's," instead of lovingly embracing them and bringing them to the feet of Jesus, which is exactly what He desires. After she sat with us for a while, another dancer also came over and sat down. We had a wonderful time and we let them pick out their Christmas presents. Then there was a woman playing pool with a customer, and after a bit came over to join us at the table. There was one other dancer who was very skeptical about even coming out to see us and receive a present and some food, but the other women said, "No, she's okay. They are both okay. Come on out." So she finally came and joined us, and oh, my word, what a Jesus party we had! It was fantastic, and I just couldn't have been more pleased. After this, we sensed it was time for us to be done. I usually stay an hour or two, and it was time.

But then Heather mentioned, "We didn't give 'S' a present." Whoa! We couldn't have that. The Lord showed me exactly what present it was to be for our new bartender friend. When "S" and I looked at each other, it was love from Jesus. She loved me, and I loved her. It was totally a gift from the Lord for both of us. She was looking outside through the window and was on the phone telling her very sad story . . . that she had cancer. The sad look on her face was so hard to watch, but I put this amazing goblet that was stunningly wrapped in iridescent eye-catching paper that had curly Q's all around it. It was a goblet from the Minnesota Renaissance Festival that had beautiful flower paintings on it, and it said, "Lady."

The bartender perfectly fit that description. She looked like a sweet, delicate lady. And I thought, how becoming! When she turned around from the window with a solemn face and looked at her present, her eyes were filled with tears. She knew Jesus loved her.

4

LEAVING HER FIRST NIGHT THERE

I don't even know how I can get through telling you the story of "J."
She was at Club #1, right around Thanksgiving, on a night Sue and I
were there. We noticed a woman who seemed extremely uncomfortable with
being at the club. She told us it was her first night, which was very easy to
believe. She kept looking over her shoulder at the dance floor and watching
the dancers perform. You could see on her face a look of, "I can't do that,"
and she told us she felt very uneasy. We have never told a woman that she
should leave the club. Our goal is that women will feel empowered and want
to leave. We can certainly encourage them, but we cannot make that decision
for them. It's one they need to make themselves.

Her story is very complex, and there were a number of things making it
difficult for her to leave this very first night of her so-called dancing career. I
will share more later about the early parts of her life. But then another dancer
whom I had come to know quite well, who had recently been encouraged
during a weekend with a group similar to AA, came over to us and talked
with "J" and said, "You can leave."

However, leaving the club was a challenge for her. Two "friends" told her
she could make a lot of money dancing at this club, and they had all come to
the club together in her car, so she was their ride home. This was toward the
beginning of the evening, around seven o'clock, and dancers had to stay until
2:00 a.m. I felt like she needed to leave, so I went over and asked the bartender
if it would be possible for her to leave without dancing. He said, "Yes, this is

not for everyone." This is such an understatement! He agreed to take the two friends home, and someone else told me they would be safe with him. So we told "J" she had permission to leave. She and I became such good friends that I became like a mother to her.

She later met a man on the internet and invited him into her life. I met him and—I hate to say it—was fooled by his appearance. You know how that song goes— "She's got legs and knows how to use them"? Well, he had big dark eyes and knew how to use them. What I didn't know was all the things that he said and did to "J" that betrayed her and showed who he really was. I thought he was a good man for her. (She had lived with a previous man and had done the best she could. She was faithful to him, but he was not faithful to her, and he was very slothful and did not help care for the two boys he fathered.)

A few months later, Jon and I were just finishing our devotions before going to bed. We were giving thanks and rejoicing about the things God was doing. At 11:30 p.m. I got a call from "J." She had never called me this late before. She was terrified and weeping, because the man who had seemingly stepped into her life to rescue her, decided to show his real colors. He had been drinking a large bottle of hard liquor which removed all restraints on his temper, which he was taking out on "J." He beat her, yanked her up from the floor by her hair, causing her great pain and emotional upheaval. He was supposed to be her rescuer, but he turned ugly. Meanwhile her little boys were screaming for him to stop hurting their mommy!

She grabbed the little ones and escaped to her car, where she was when she called me and told me what happened. She did not want to inconvenience me by having me drive an hour to go pick her up, because when she was growing up she had always been told she was a burden. After reasoning with her for over an hour on the phone, and trying to calm her down, I told her I would not sleep at all until I brought her safely to my home. Only after I told her the Lord had told me to go and pick her up, did she agree to let me come. The next day we made a police report, and the man was arrested and put in jail for a few days.

My head is still swirling from all the things that occurred. It was amazing I was even able to drive to go pick her up, and it was close to 2:00 a.m. by the time I got there. I told her not to go back into that apartment to get diapers for the boys. I said, "If you go in there, you will come out on a stretcher. Please do not go back into that apartment." So she came home with me, and we had quite a time trying to find diapers at 2:30 a.m. in the morning. It was a horrific, tumultuous night. How could any of us sleep after what we had been through?

The next day she felt she had to go back to her place, but only after we filed the police report. It was amazing. I sat nearby while she talked to the police officer. She did not want to tell the full truth about the story because she had such low self-esteem that she could not even put the blame on this man for doing what he did. It was an intentional act of violence against her, which certainly could have ended in her death.

It's hard to go through all the events that have happened in the past two years of my ongoing friendship and motherhood to my sweet "J." I love her so much. We still talk a lot, and I did get to see her recently for a short visit. She met another man on the internet, which of course terrified me. I was very, very skeptical after her last experience. They ended up getting married, which was a delightful thing. It was a very quiet wedding, just the two of them before a justice of the peace. She has since given birth to her heart's desire—a little girl, her little princess.

5

"GO IN!"

My sweet mentor, Renee, began gently nudging me out of my comfort zone. She gave me a Wisconsin map, on which she had circled the two clubs that she wanted me to go into. A visual that became fixed in my mind. And so it was almost exactly two years later, after my entrance into the club nearest to me, that I fearfully entered Club #2. The day went like this. Jon and I were driving two hours from home that day to meet some friends coming up from the South. I had brought my face paints along, and I painted the faces of this couple's sweet children. We had a wonderful time of fellowship with them.

We then headed toward home, and realizing that Club #2 was on our route, I said to Jon, "Should we go in the parking lot of this club that Renee had circled? Should we pray to see if I should tiptoe in and ask permission to come there in the future?" This place is quite different from Club #1. I forget what it is called when women beat the men, but that happens in this club. (I might add that I have never, in the more than seven years I have been going there, seen or heard anything that would indicate this club had that activity going on). Jon and I drove up and parked in the parking lot. Then we prayed. "Lord, is this the time for me to make my initial contact?" Then Jon said, "What do you think?" And I said, "I don't know. I'm too nervous to be able to hear from God. I think we'll have to flip a coin." Sometimes when we have big decisions to make, we flip a coin. So we prayed, flipped the coin, and the Lord said, "Go in!" Of course I was terrified, but I knew it was God.

I went inside and saw a female bartender that I would really come to love. Her name is "J." When I walked in, she was behind this long bar, and I had forgotten that I had painted a Fall design on my face. It was a pumpkin with a vine curled around it, and a very large butterfly on the other side, but I thought, "Hey, why not? This is not your everyday place." When I sat down, "J" came toward me and I introduced myself, then asked her if I could bring the dancers some homemade soaps as presents. I thought, "Well, if this flies, it's got to be God." She hesitated, smiled and then told me her name. (She's never told me her real name, but someone else did.) She reached out to shake my hand and said, "Yes, you can." I was so elated, I could barely control my emotions. Across from the bar was one of the dancers named "H." ("H" and I are still good friends, and we have messaged each other quite frequently.) She looked at me and said, "Hi, I'm 'H.' I love your face painting." I replied, "I can paint this on you too." She told me the nights she worked, and I knew the bartender "J" was working on Thursday nights. So I said to myself, "Thursday night, it is." I already had permission from this bartender who works on Thursday night and the dancer confirmed that that was one of her nights. Bingo. So when I went back out to the car, I was beside myself with joy, and Jon and I rejoiced greatly!

6

"LET'S HAVE A CELEBRATION"

C lub #2 is truly an unusual bar. Occasionally I have seen scenes from the television program, "Cheers," but you wouldn't expect a venue where women beat the men to be a place where there would be comradery between the customers and the dancers.

Most of the volunteers could not afford or find time for the three-hour round trip to this destination. But Brianna started coming with me because she had a heart for this type of ministry, and she could handle the long distance. Where I live now is actually a half an hour further.

We started visiting near Thanksgiving time. One night while Brianna and I sat at our little table with our food and presents surrounding us, I was having a conversation with "J," one of the young dancers. She was telling us how she was raised in low-income housing, and that it's not a nice place to grow up. Then from across the room, one of the other dancers walked to our spot and said, "I'm not comfortable with you being here." I thought, "Now isn't this interesting" — there she was far away, and she walked all the way over into our little section to tell us that she wasn't comfortable with our being there! Well, believe it or not, I took it in stride, and she walked away to the opposite end of the bar. It's quite a long bar. The Lord had me go to the other end and start talking to her, and He poured out His love for this amazing woman.

Actually, "J" wasn't even working that night, so she had no make-up on. But when the Lord started pouring His love out verbally through my mouth, she started telling me what a creep she was. I can't even remember the derogatory way she described herself. Everything was terribly, terribly negative. And I couldn't believe she could say all those awful things about herself. The Lord had me put my two hands around her face and tell her how beautiful she was, how talented she was and how much the Lord loved her. She did not know how to respond. Tears cascaded down her face. It was Jesus! He was showing her how precious she was.

I had some amazing conversations with "J" after our initial encounter. She was there as a dancer one night when Brianna and I were there. I saw her and said, "Hi," and she responded in a mellow voice, "Dotty, I've just finished my nursing degree. I've graduated." But she said it with very little emotion, like it was nothing to celebrate. Now, mind you, where she graduated from is a university that has very high standards and is quite costly. I got so excited that she had graduated from this amazingly prestigious university. I looked around and everyone knew it, but no one was celebrating. I said, "What's wrong with this? We should be celebrating. We should be giving you a party." But, of course, I couldn't do it that night because I had not known her graduation had happened, but she was very encouraged by my excitement.

The next time I came she was there as well. I talked more about her talent, her degree, and what her aspirations were. But her hopes were unachievable in her mind. I said, "No, honey, you can do it. You can do it." She told me she had three job offers. By this time she was texting me, which was very exciting. She said, "Dotty, I'm not going to get any of these jobs because I have two counts against me, one for prostitution and the other for drunk driving." I replied, "Honey, this is a different time. People are now aware of the way many, many women are forced into sexual slavery or prostitution. It will be okay. It will be okay. And Brianna and I, and our prayer team, will be praying for you."

Thank you, Jesus, who walks with us into these dark places. "J" texted me later and said she had several job offers, but she wanted to be accepted at the most prestigious of these, which I was 100% in favor of. After she received the job she longed for, I saw her once more in person at the club. She wept and said, "Dotty, it's because of you and your team that I've got this job." I couldn't believe it. Jesus is so amazing in how He can use simple human beings without much training, but are just open to His heart, and use us in such a magnificent way. I mean, wow, this is awesome.

After she left the club, I met her cousin who was still working there. I hadn't had much bonding with the cousin, but the good news is that she let me know how "J" was doing from time to time, and that she did take this job. However, "J" stopped texting me completely, and I think the reason is because it was a part of her past she did not want to be reminded anymore.

It's heartbreaking to not have contact with her anymore, but a total joy to know that we were instrumental in her getting the job. I later found out from her cousin she took that job and worked there for a while, and was well accepted and received. Then she chose a more local place to work because she was traveling such a long distance. So it was all good except, oh my, how I wish we still had contact.

7

OUT OF THE DARK CORNERS

When Jon and I made our first trip to the Philippines in 2004, our original goal was to visit a number of Filipino brethren who gathered in homes, but we ended up starting the trip working with a ministry in Quezon City that helped women get out of prostitution. The workers were humble, highly trained Filipino women. The morning after we arrived we were shown a brief documentary telling how women were forced into sexual slavery. Many were sold, tricked or guilted into supplying income for their families. An interesting thing happens when these women succumb to selling themselves as sexual slaves. The families who forced them into this slavery then suddenly turn their backs on their children, and view them as "dirty."

Jon and I realized these women did not get into the sex trade by choice, but had mental or physical trauma that pushed them into sexual slavery on the streets or in strip clubs. The bars in the Philippines are all connected to prostitution. We went out on the streets with one of the skilled ministry women, and I was very nervous that the sex workers would be hesitant to accept me and Jon. The bar women were not allowed to infringe on the "territory" of the street women, and vice-versa. Almost all of them were owned by pimps. As we were walking along with Tina, this delightful sister in the Lord, we could see what a heart she had for these marginalized women.

While we were on the streets with her, the women would appear from the darker corners and come to her like bees to honey. Oh, my word, Jon and I were thrilled that they were not afraid of us being very large Americans compared to these little Filipinos. But I think some of it is a leftover from World War II when we came to the aid of the Philippines so that the country was not conquered. When we stood with Tina in those darker spots, it was such a joy to see how comfortable the women felt sharing their hearts with her. My heart sank when a customer would come along and Tina knew she would have to let them go. I couldn't believe it, knowing what could happen to these women after they left us. I didn't even want to think about whether or not they would come back in one piece. But that was Tina's approach to working with these women. She had to release them into God's hands.

Jon and I could only do this for a few days because we were also visiting other ministries and had quite a tight schedule. However, we had a couple of extra days at the end of our three weeks, and both of us heartily agreed to go back and work with this outreach. I ended up going to the Philippines four times, twice with Jon, and twice with others, staying for three or four weeks each time.

Later, I ended up working with a ministry in Angeles City, where the strip clubs started during WWII near a US military base. At that time, prostitution became — I hate to even utter the word — commonplace. You would think after the war was over those places would close down, but they did not. It not only continued, but increased significantly. In 2009, 30% of Angeles City's income was from the sex industry. The ministry's focus was on the karaoke bars and strip clubs. The street lined by all these bars was several miles long, and called "Friendship Street," and we were able to experience different kinds of sex clubs, both small and very large.

We ended up mostly going to one particular big club, because one of the young Filipino women who had come out and found freedom in Christ, had a cousin who worked as a stripper there. This club had thirty or forty women on the stage. It was so horrific. The women had numbers pinned on them, so they didn't even have the dignity of a name, and people could view all of these women on the large stage. It was like the old fashioned, very large movie theaters with a balcony, or like a music venue with a second floor. And you could see the women moving about very subtly. You could tell it was not in their comfort zone to do this activity. There was a Mamason or a Papason in charge. A Mamason was like a dorm mother, and would keep the women in line. A Papason was a male figure who would keep the women obedient. And the place was packed with maybe two hundred people. If a customer decided they wanted to take a certain young woman, the Mamason or Papason pointed a little red laser light at the number on the woman the person had asked for.

I was with a friend, Bonnie, on that particular trip, but she and I were not sitting right next to each other. The music there was very loud, so I could not hear the conversation that Bonnie heard. There were young women dancers in the row in front of us who were laughing and joking around. I just thought that was so strange. However, I later found out that a foreign customer had picked one of their friends to take to the nearby hotel, and he was from a country where the men tended to be violent. So when this girl was chosen, her friends accompanied her as far as they could. Then they had to let her go with the customer into the hotel, hoping she would return in one piece. In this particular case, she did. She was not hurt very much and did not experience any of the horrific things that could have happened, such as being drugged, beaten or murdered. So these dancers were all laughing and celebrating because their friend was okay. This was a life-altering experience for me.

After I went back to the States, Jon and I were introduced to an awesome group that I became part of, Whispered Hopes because "God hears our whispered hopes." Renee, the founding volunteer, became my mentor. Months later, with Renee's encouragement, Jon and I saw the documentary, "Nefarious: Merchant of Souls," produced by Exodus Cry. We were horrified at the extent of human trafficking, especially in America. As far as I'm concerned, it is absolutely a must-see account of the sex industry worldwide.

It takes the viewers through five continents, showing different aspects of human trafficking and human slavery. The opening scenes are horrific. I wanted to run and turn it off and just say, "I cannot watch this." However, we were in a large-screen movie theater, so we had to sit through it. It ventures through one country after another, with the last place they focused on being the United States. You may be thinking, "this is the United States; this does not happen here." Much to our chagrin, the U.S. is one of the worst places for sexual tourism, which involves people traveling to other countries for the purpose of abusing children and adults. What you discover through watching this documentary is that even though there are millions of dollars spent on rescuing women, girls, and even boys, a huge percentage of this population goes back into sexual slavery within one year. One big reason for this is shame. The really good news is that when you come to Jesus and he cleanses you from your shame, you can walk in newness of life.

8

CONSEQUENCES OF BURIED TRAUMA

At the beginning of my experience of going into strip clubs I had assumed that the dancers would not be followers of Jesus. However, that is not true. When Renee first told me that some of these women are Jesus followers, I didn't believe her. I did not think it was possible, but it is. I've met some women who actually love Jesus, but they are trapped in their circumstances. Their last chapter is not written yet. One of the women I am closest to, who loves Jesus, was raised in her grandmother's house. This house had six garages, and this was a long time ago, when people were fortunate to have one garage. When I saw the lineup of garages, one would wonder what was going on here.

This young woman, who became a very close friend, invited me into her grandmother's house, that had been built long ago. When you walk in, you see a professional bar, not like one of those cute little bars some people have in their homes, but an old-fashioned solid oak bar. Across from the bar there was the large, thick metal door of a walk-in safe. The young woman took me inside what was a room where the money was kept. I never got to see the upstairs, but I do know this treasured friend of mine grew up in this house, and that her mother was an alcoholic. I discovered this house was used during Prohibition for bootlegging moonshine.

When this particular friend of mine told me she was not sexually abused as a child, I almost fell over, because I know there's a good chance she was sold by her grandmother, and maybe even her mother, I don't know.

I was molested as a child for several years. I don't know exactly how old I was. My grandfather lived with us during my early childhood. I think I might've been three, four or five when he molested me. He also molested my mother and my Aunt Kay, who raised me. I'm not sure if he molested Aunt Helen, who may have been in cooperation with her father. He beat and sodomized his son so badly that he ran away from home at age twelve.

So I understand how you can block that out of your mind, because of the shame, and the fact that you may have been sexually abused as a child. I was around thirty-eight when I was able to cope with the fact I had been sexually abused by him. It was another ten years before I discovered he also sodomized me. I used to watch the movie "Prince of Tides." What an emotionally compelling movie it is! There's a scene in which one of the two men finds out he was sodomized as a child, when the psychologist in a climactic moment unearths the memory of his life-shattering violation.

Later in life, I realized I went through a similar trauma as a young child. When I watched this movie I would cry and cry during that scene. I rationalized, "At least I wasn't sodomized," until one day the Lord said, "It's time; now you need to acknowledge this happened to you." This was another whole level of healing for me. I bless the Lord for the healers in my life—compassionate, amazing healers. The Lord is good. Although I would never wish any kind of sexual trauma on a child or an adult, I realized if that had not happened to me, I would never have been emotionally enabled to go into strip clubs. I would not have understood the emotions behind the betrayal. I understand why women and girls choose to leave their home when they are traumatized by relatives. They would rather be on the streets than risk the trauma encountered at home.

We know this is wrong. It should never happen. Our families should be safe places. In my home, my aunt Kay raised me, along with my precious grandma, but my aunt was a very angry woman. She was angry because her father molested her. She buried that and paid many consequences, one of which was having a nervous breakdown. Aunt Kay was very controlling and never let me have a will of my own. I was to be silent. Whatever I did, it was not good enough, and she yelled at me a lot.

At the time I had no clue why she was so angry at me. My grandfather's molestations also greatly affected my mother. When I was very young, my mother had repeated nervous breakdowns because she could not acknowledge what had happened to her. Being in this state, she could not raise me, and ultimately, Aunt Kay had my mom committed to a mental institution. When I was roughly between the ages of two to twelve my mom was locked up. In those days, when a person went into a mental institution, it was very difficult for them to get out. The movie, "One Flew Over the Cuckoo's Nest," was a lifesaver for me. It helped me understand why my mother was always judged by many people as wacko and out of her mind. Her trauma was compounded by the fact she could not talk about the abuse, and the worst part was not being able to say, "This happened to me," and be taken seriously.

Because of my own denial, it took me a long time to recover from my abuse. The Lord sent some wonderful healers into my life who helped me walk through my sexual trauma. Grandma was Jesus to me. Grandma brought everything to the Lord. She was a woman of few words, but she was my rock. Grandma loved me, and I knew it. Sometimes Grandma could not defend me, and I'm sure she had to be in a lot of denial herself. She was from the old school where women couldn't protect their young from abuse by men. Fortunately, in her case, her husband divorced her. That was the background of my childhood, and the foundation of my growing experience in the world of sexual slavery.

9

"OPENING NIGHT"

U p to this point, almost all of the Whispered Hopes team were more mature women, with the exception of two who were in their younger or early twenties, and they ended up moving to a large city. One of them continued to have a heavy burden to reach club women. A team emerged from the church she attended, and after much prayer, they selected a club to visit. Since it was more of a metropolis, the club would be more hardcore. Therefore, Renee and I felt a desire to come alongside them on their first visit to the club.

I was very excited about this trip, since I had already experienced "opening night" at my local club. So I felt emboldened and forged to the head of our little troop as we asked permission to enter the club as a Whispered Hopes team, which they gave us. I was actually there two different times. We had a very good reception with the dancers and the bartender. She was also what would be considered a "house mother" for the club dancers. From my understanding, some of the women who didn't have living quarters resided in a house near the club and were watched over by this "house mother." She was a bit older, and she very joyfully received us into the club.

I have to tell you how awesome this particular ministry is in this large city. The young mom who started this ministry, formerly part of the Whispered Hopes team, is part of a large church that is very aware of the connection between human trafficking and strip clubs, and desired to help this new team develop. This little team would go to a coffee shop and catch up on what was going on in their lives. If there were six or eight women, half of them would stay at the coffee shop and pray the entire time the others went into the club, waiting for their return. When they came back they would give a report of what the Lord had done that night. I just love this. And it is no wonder they are seeing fantastic things happen.

This concerned group of women would show their love by putting together beautiful presents for the dancers. I happened to be there on one of those occasions, and it was precious.

On one of the two nights I had my face paints with me, there was a young woman who came and had me paint on her midsection, then she went to the dance floor. After a while she came back and wanted me to paint some more, which I was thrilled to do. This happened four times, and the last time I happened to notice there was something strange about one area of her midriff. I asked her what it was. She told me it was the name of her boyfriend that she had had since she was fourteen years old. His name had been stitched into her skin! Fortunately, very often when something very shocking happens at the club, I don't process it right away. It's after I leave that it dawns on me what had actually happened to her. I realized this was his trademark of ownership. Needless to say, this was horrifying and demonstrated the fact that she was owned by this pimp and has been from the time she was fourteen. Sadly, she considers him to be her boyfriend. When a pimp owns more than one sex slave, it is called a "corral."

The horrors I have seen over the years in the strip clubs only underscores the importance of reaching out to these women and bringing them the hope of Jesus.

10

WE CANNOT BE CONDESCENDING

Renee will be embarrassed to see I added this to my story, but I love working with Renee who started Whispered Hopes, and invited me into this ministry. She is so calm and collected. When I get upset about not having the time to bake the bread I love to bring to the women at the club, she settles me down and says, "It's all right." And she is so correct. God uses us anyway. It's not so much about us, but about Jesus and His light shining through us. It's about us all being equal before a holy God, all sinners until the light of Christ breaks through our darkness. So thank you, Renee, for being who you are in Christ and a wonderful follower of Him, even in the darkness of the strip bar scene. Isn't it beautiful and amazing that the darkness is dispelled by light? Darkness has to flee when the Light shines through, and it is thrilling God has chosen me to be a participant in this ministry. I love it.

11

SURPRISES AND FLEXIBILITY

I always get excited when I go to a club to meet with our friends, and show them Jesus through love. Speaking very little, but listening, listening, listening. We'll usually wait for them to ask why we came bringing presents, food and hugs. I think they know in their hearts what brings us to love on them.

This particular night was a long one for me. The original plan was to go to the club where I was being trained. By the time I had spent one and a half hours driving to Renee's, and then another forty-five minutes to arrive at this particular club, only to discover locked doors, you can imagine my dismay at not seeing these women I have come to love. Renee offered to drive another half hour to the other club I was training at. By then it was a late start, around 7:30 p.m., when typically, we start at the club around 5 p.m. We left the club to arrive at Renee's at 10 p.m., and I eventually arrived back home at 1:00 a.m. Long night, but worth every minute.

I used to have a goal of face painting each woman in the club, but this particular night was so good, and I only painted four of my friends. Our friendships are growing to the point where each encounter with these lovely women is weaving a tapestry of love. The complexity of their lives and ours are becoming intertwined. God's wisdom is so beyond our understanding. It is so amazing. So wonderful. I sit in awe that God has chosen me for this utterly delightful mission, and has allowed me to partake in it. Thank you,

Jesus, and thank you, all of my unseen prayer warriors who participate in breaking down strongholds in spiritual realms. Jesus is the king!

12

IN IT FOR THE LONG HAUL

Heaven and hell. That's what the clubs are. Heaven is when Jesus brings His life into the club through us. Hell is what the women who dance have to go through night after night. And that's just the little I know. The way our friends are charged to do their work was revealed during one visit. A VIP dance costs the customer $30. Only $20 goes to the dancer, and $10 goes to the club. It makes me sick to my stomach! And, unbelievably, in some clubs they are also charged for their dance floor space each night! ,

On the bright side of our visit, Brianna and I were so encouraged to have more in-depth conversations with those women who had spent a lot of time with us in the past. The first night I was there, one beautiful young woman took a long time before she was willing to come out and talk to us because she thought we were Bible pushers, bringing condemnation. But by the time the night was over she was freely chatting with us. When we exited through the dance area, and we waved goodbye to her, she left the person she was giving special attention to on the stage, walked downstage to us and gave us a big hug, thanking us profusely for coming to be with them that night. She spent a lot of time talking and sharing her life with us.

Another dear woman who I still have amazing contact with said, "I'll stop what I'm doing with so-and-so and hug my friends, Brianna and Dotty, goodbye." She gave us her phone number and told us she'd like to get together, which would include her little girl. Brianna told her how much money she made at a local restaurant, and our dancer friend was seriously considering working there instead. She had encountered a lot of opposition at the club because some men who were high on drugs came in one night, and they were sitting in front of her, when one fell backwards off of his chair with his eyes rolled up in his head. At that point my dancing friend exclaimed out loud, "Drugs!" It wasn't too long afterwards that she was forced out of that club. Dancers already feel like they are in hell, but being kicked out of a club sends them the message that they are not even good enough for hell! "You're so evil. You're so bad." That's the feeling they get.

The good news is that when I saw her later, she excitedly told me she got a job at a different club. Of course, that didn't exactly thrill me, until she told me that she now worked half the hours and made more money than she did at the previous club. Years later, she started a lucrative dog grooming business. Oh, how I love this woman!

Jesus is bringing so much light into that place. Several of our friends said over and over how much they appreciated our coming. It was amazing. We were so thankful God brought us to this place where His love is shining brighter and brighter, and our relationships are getting stronger and stronger.

Jesus, thank You for allowing us to be Your light in such an otherwise dark place. And thank You for protecting us and letting us soak up Your presence the whole time we are there.

Many times I think about how we are going into these dark places. And what happens? The women are so grateful for the food and gifts we bring them. But they love our presence with them most of all, that we want to be with them, love them, care for them, and that we truly love them down from the depths of our hearts. It's so awesome. Sometimes I really feel very spoiled in such a good way. I think what really has the greatest impact on them is that they see we are in this with them for the long haul.

13

FRIENDS AND CONVERSATION

O ur new friend ran out waving at us for a hug. We embraced for quite a while and chatted like we were old friends. She talked about her ex-husband who was extremely bad to her and her children. She talked freely about trying to find a church where she and her three kids would feel comfortable in. They finally found one they all loved, and her children were very involved. We talked so freely about Jesus and His magnificent love and care for us. It just seemed to be such a weird place to have such great conversations.

There were actually two women we had deep Jesus interactions with. After a while they both disappeared, and I am very sure their disappearances were a very good thing. I think they both left the club scene for new lives with Jesus and are well on their way to finding new directions for themselves and their children.

14

"I THINK I'M GETTING TO KNOW THE LORD"

I 'll have to tell you some later developments that happened after our first visit to Club #1. The bartender there had told us about some health issues, and I had given her that beautiful chalice that had "Lady" inscribed on it. We had become very good friends with her, and she was recovering from the flu and surgery, which we later learned was for cancer. Last month she told Heather and I she had numerous cysts inside her body, at least one of which was probably inoperable, and she looked frail.

I gave her my first loaf of bread and also a small decorative handmade bar of goat milk soap. It was made by a close friend of mine. It was actually very cool because one time I milked the goat, whose milk went into making the soaps that she had donated for the women. And it was also a lot of fun, just making it part of my ministry with my friend.

After some time this bartender who we had become very close to quit. She got angry at something, and she ended up going down the street to another bar. It was just a regular bar, and had no strippers. On a couple of different occasions I went with one of my co-laborers into it to visit her, and they were wonderful times. I am sure this bartender came to know the Lord. I think she had a Catholic background. She didn't use any of the usual religious terms many of us are familiar with, but she said something like, "I think I'm getting to know the Lord more." We kept on seeing more and more positives coming out of our talks with her. She is such a dear friend.

As our custom was, I met my co-worker, Cheryl, in the parking lot of the bar down the street. Then we left one of the cars there, and she and I hopped into the other car and went to Club #1. Something very strange happened that day. There is a liquor store attached to the same building as that bar, and while Cheryl and I were sitting there in the car chatting and catching up, a huge bus pulled into the parking lot, and some people got out. Men went into the liquor store on Sunday and came back out with liquor. Another interesting thing also happened. There was a police officer who waved them on. He was standing outside of the bus. It looked like he was giving them permission to continue on their route. He was not pulling them over to question them as far as we could see. It almost looked like he was friends with them. Now this whole circumstance is very odd as Cheryl and I have reflected on it because there's nothing else on this street, since it had almost become a dead end. It made us think that bus had something to do with going to the strip club we were about to enter. Bizarre indeed.

15

BARTENDERS AND BOUNCERS

E veryone has their own personality. After I had come to love the first bartender, she quit this club and went to work at a nearby bar. The next bartender at this club was surprisingly a very normal looking, modestly dressed young woman, and I loved her too. She had to leave after a while because she became deathly allergic to wheat, and had to stop working.

After her came a young male bartender who was very skeptical of us. His name was "D." He thought at first we were religious Bible-thumping, finger-pointing women, but after some time he realized we really cared about these women, and we were not there to preach at them, but just to love on them. So he began to accept us and he became, in a loose way, like a son to me. Once I made him an upside down rhubarb cake for his birthday. Unfortunately, he had an emergency come up that night, and he was not there. We ended up visiting the club another night when he was working. Six women were dancing. Three were old friends of ours and three new. All six of them spent a lot of time with us as we enjoyed our Jesus party together. I had been given some lovely clothes and scarves by a friend, and the women were shocked and thrilled when I told them the items were free. And we were just as happy as they were. They thanked us over and over. We had some intimate glimpses into their lives, which thrilled us beyond measure. There was an atmosphere of acceptance coming into that place and the women felt free to share their lives with us.

It took a new bouncer a long time to trust us. Later, we became very good friends. I showed him a painting I had just done of the Father holding His son in His arms, who had run away and was now returning (The Prodigal Son). He loved it so much that I told him I'd give him a copy for his birthday. Then I thought about how life is short and things change a lot in this environment, so I gave it to him early, which made him so happy.

Both the bartender and the bouncer had custody of their children. I tend to think of women as being the motherly ones who care for their children, but in this case, both of these men were raising their kids. God was showing me there are caring men who are raising their children.

16

BEAUTIFUL AS A PURE BRIDE

Something happened on one visit that was really cool. We had expected to visit with the women, which was our usual habit. I think there was one woman dancing this particular night. By this time Karlie was coming with me, and God's plan that night was to spend time alone with the bartender. He came over to our table and spent almost the entire time with Karlie and I without interruptions. "D" told us a lot of his history, some of which was extremely painful to him. He had tried to visit me at a thrift store I volunteered at, but the day he came, I was not there. Every time this bartender was working and Karlie was with me, he could not take his eyes off of Karlie, which wasn't surprising because she was drop dead gorgeous. It's very fascinating how the Lord sometimes has me bringing the most beautiful women into this club scene. And I'm thinking, "Lord, what are You doing?" But the thing about Karlie — and I'm sure this would embarrass her to tears, but it's true – she was a picture of the bride of Christ. Some of the women who dance are very attractive, some average, and others not that attractive. Enter Karlie. She was a picture of purity, and she was just as sweet as she could be. The bartender told us some of the other male customers were mesmerized by Karlie. The truth, of course, was Karlie was not for sale. Karlie had been bought by the blood of Jesus, and she's a bond servant to the living God.

17

A RUSHING WIND

This was certainly an interesting experience. Jon and I were driving near Club #1, and I asked him if I could stop by for a few minutes so I could let the women know that I would be coming a little bit later that night. When I entered, the presence of God was so strong I literally felt the rushing wind. What was this about? Joy was everywhere as I hugged the women dancers and the bartender. The plan was for us to return an hour or two later.

I looked at the names of the five dancers that were scheduled that night, and there was one I had become very close to. As it turned out the rushing wind that I felt was right before this dancer left this club permanently. It was really amazing, but I didn't really understand what was happening until I walked out. Then I realized, wow, that was like the beginning of Acts. She didn't have much time to talk to us because she was on a mission to save money, so she could move out of her present location and away from her abusive relationship, which I was very happy to hear. I usually never do this, but I actually gave her some money to help her with the down payment on another place.

One of the women said how thankful she was that we came and listened to them because she knew the men really didn't care about them, or want to hear about their lives.

When I first went in, I brought a huge wicker picnic basket I bought at a garage sale. One particular young woman was admiring it. I decided the first one who commented on it would get it. So this woman loved it, and I said, "It's yours." To me, it appeared she was pimped, so I was tickled she received this lovely gift.

I also decided at this time to give out "God Hears our Whispered Hopes" pins to every woman that night. Each woman not only received the pin, but wore them on their person that very night, and I read the verse from the Psalms to each person. The bartender put hers on her leather jacket. God is at work.

Got home again around 11:45 p.m., exhausted, mostly thinking about the strong possibility some of these new women were being trafficked. I may never see them again, which is why I felt so strongly I was to personally present them with their only hope, who is Jesus.

18

LIFE CAN BE HARD

The male bartender friend, "D," who was like a son to me, was having a very hard time dealing with the recent death of his younger brother. This brother died in a motorcycle accident when he was riding it while drunk. The bartender had a tender heart, had rescued his brother many times before, and begged him to stop drinking and driving. He also told me about a time when there was a missing child, and authorities called for many volunteers to comb the area to look for the child, and "D" was one of the volunteers. I thought what an amazing man this is. They later found the child dead in the trunk of a car. It was very, very sad, to say the least.

19

"ANGELED" EGGS

In October, 2014, Brianna and I walked into Club #2, which was over two hours away. The Lord did it again through the prayer and fasting of our sisters and brothers. To my surprise, the bouncer recognized me from my introductory visit the Thursday night before, and he mentioned I did not have my face painted tonight.

The female bartender and I were soon to become close friends. She was so friendly to us and delighted that we brought "angeled" eggs. Now, I have to tell you about angeled eggs. Other people call them "deviled" eggs, but anything that delicious, I did not think the devil should get any credit for. So I renamed them "angeled" eggs. The women loved the new name and many times would ask me if I was bringing angeled eggs. The bartender let us place the eggs behind the bar, where we had also put homemade soup, and small gift candles for each dancer. The fact we were given permission to go behind the bar was amazing to me, truly a sign Jesus had given us authority in that place.

We had in-depth conversations with two dancers, a mother and daughter. They really seem to have a good relationship with each other. Both of them not only gave us their dancing names, but their real names as well. When this happens, I feel extremely honored, and that we have a special relationship with them where they trust us enough to give us their actual names. This is an obvious indication God is working ahead of our arrival. The irony is that this mom and daughter were active in a Pentecostal church!

Another dancer told us she has a six-year-old daughter who had a birthday the next day. A customer gave her a present for her daughter. One of the dancers didn't come over to our table, but was very friendly. She always had a male client. All the women gave us multiple hugs, and thanked us profusely for the eggs, the chocolate and the candles. It was very obvious God was answering our prayers.

We were given permission by my wonderful bartender friend to return. Yay! Our plan was to celebrate Thanksgiving with them in the middle of November, Lord willing. I arrived home around midnight, exhausted but exhilarated. Thank you so much for holding us up during our long journey home through fog—two deer were spotted on the side of the road.

20

COMING TO OUR JESUS TABLE

I remember the night I brought the women items with which to make miniature fairy gardens. That was a lot of fun. The bartender was kind of tickled and worked on her miniature garden at our table. A dancer I knew well was going to take her mini garden home to work on with her little daughter. One of the men was following her around most of the evening. Several nights I observed this. She had told me that to be a success, you have to enter your customer's mind and figure out what his fantasy is, and this particular dancer knew how to do that. Her customer patiently waited for her, and watched her creativity, as she played around with her little garden. I brought a "My Little Pony" as one of the centerpieces, and she had a lot of fun with that. I got a kick out of her customer allowing her to play with it, just watching her intently. A new woman was a school bus driver, and she spent quite a bit of time with Karlie. She had a six-year-old little girl, and she was the dancer who was going to recreate this mini-garden at home.

Two men were very interested in our work there, and they were quite surprised that the gifts and food were all given freely to these women. One man followed me around quite a bit, fascinated with how these women have our hearts. Karlie and I were quite disappointed because of a slow start, but we realized we did have some nice conversations before we left. I have to remind myself that the ease with which the women came to our table and spent time with us isn't an ordinary thing. It is to be taken and received as a gift from the Lord.

Karlie and I sat in my car after we were done, and I told her how passionate I am about throwing out a lifeline to the women in this dark area, where there is no one else we know of bringing in the light of Jesus. I'm honored to be able to bring Jesus there and hopefully see some of them reach out to the anchor of their souls. Their only hope is Jesus. After years working alongside these women in the clubs, I have been very excited to hear that there are other women like us in other clubs in various parts of the States.

21

GOD EVEN USES FLEAS

I send out prayer letters to a team of prayer warriors, who stand with us, and who go in with us (figuratively speaking) to the clubs. They are a vital part of this ministry, and I thank them deeply. You are reading the stumbling thoughts of a feeble woman who by the grace of God is as bold as a lion, because that's who Jesus makes us to be. It's so fulfilling when we find our place in this world, the mission God has for us, and includes mothers who choose to stay home and raise citizens for the next generation. This also includes workers who are cleaning toilets, those who are working hard out in the fields, sweating so they can provide for their families. We don't even want to go into the horrific thoughts, but it is true of migrant workers who do not perhaps even get to eat from the labor of their hands. "Lord, Lord, help them find You, give them food and drink and let them drink abundantly from Your reservoir which has no bottom. You are unfathomable. You are everything they need. Lord help them."

As in Psalm 23, we reside by still waters, wherever we are. I so often think of Corrie ten Boom, that beloved precious saint who was captive in a horrific prison with her sister, Betsy. Betsy had such strong faith. She died in the prison, but she died in the arms of Jesus. And she lived in the arms of Jesus every day. I cannot forget a part of Corrie's book, The Hiding Place. There were fleas, and they were such an annoyance to them. The fleas were constant, bugging them, no pun intended. And later on, Betsy said, "My dear Corrie, don't you realize it's because of the fleas the soldiers do not come in here and harass us all the time. God can use the things that are so irksome. We wish they were different, but God can use them to dissuade the enemy from coming after us."

On another night, the ladies spent time finding treasures from the blouses, purses and cosmetic bags we brought them. Brianna and I had a ball with the women as they tried on various blouses or dresses to find just the right one for them. Our food that night was grilled cheese and bacon sandwiches. Just as we departed, the bartender thanked us again for coming. Does it get any better than this? The bartender led applause for our coming. Can you believe it? As we exited, she had everyone who was sitting at the bar, including the women dancers, applaud us for coming! This happened several times when we were in Club #2. Talk about Jesus giving us hugs! It was awesome. One of the dancers said she knows our secret — we are really angels in disguise. I am telling you this ministry has moments of great joy, which are so fulfilling. I know it's what Jesus has led me to do, and I hope to be doing it for a long time.

22

"THIS CAN'T BE THE RIGHT PLACE!"

An art show in St. Paul, Minnesota, changed my life. Jon and I were on a mission to find the venue where my former dancer friend's artwork was being highlighted. "B" left the club the first night I met her. She was now holding a fundraiser to earn money to see her children up north. As we were traveling, I said to Jon, "the GPS says we are almost there, but it can't be right!" This was a rundown neighborhood. We drove into this large parking lot and I thought, "there's no way." When we ventured to the end of the parking lot, we saw the address was correct. It was a hairdresser's salon, and it was hosting the art show. Still very skeptical, we walked in the door. Other than us, there were very few people in the room. The owner, who specialized in African braids, said, "this is the place." We looked around at the ex-dancer's artwork.

A few minutes later we sat down because a program was starting. It was only us and a few in the audience. Then two little children did a short recital. The front of this venue had been made into a small stage. There was a man who was leaning over with a black top coat on, fine tuning some audio equipment for his one-man play. It was a very powerful performance.

Following that, we purchased one of her paintings, which was extremely reasonable. She's such an amazing, tender-hearted person. In her job up north, she wasn't making very much money, so she decided to go out West to work with her dad in construction. For me, her moving was very sad because that's the last time I heard from her. She may have lost her phone or maybe it was stolen, thus losing all her contacts. We have moved twice since she was in our home. Nevertheless, I have hopes she is a Jesus lover. So I left her in God's hands, even though her absence broke my heart.

23

"HAPPY BIRTHDAY!" TWICE

O ne of my favorite memories happened on my 70th birthday celebration. I said to my husband, "This year, I want to have two birthday parties, one in each of my two clubs." Jon chuckled, "Of course that's what my wife would want to do." For Club #2, I made the best cheesecake I've ever made! I just have to tell you how cool this is.

Since it was my birthday, I wasn't going to put 70 candles on the cake, but I did put quite a few on it. I was actually standing behind the bar, because the Lord gave us authority there. Someone lit the candles for us, and the girls joyfully hovered around me. Now, at that time, it was almost like the atmosphere of the TV hit "Cheers." I've only seen it a few times, but it's like a friendly neighborhood bar kind of scene. They had many of the same customers who actually seemed to care for the women. The dancers and all the customers were watching this celebration. One of the men at the bar was so excited about me having my party with the women that he took out his camera to photograph the exciting occasion. I blew the candles out and he took a picture that was totally fuzzy. He was drunk. We all got a big kick out of that. So we lit the candles again, and the same guy took a picture. Same result! By this time we were all in the complete stitches! So one of the women said, "I'll take the picture." By this time we were having such a blast that even my favorite bartender came running over to get her face in the picture, because they knew this picture was safe with us. Oh, my word, how precious that was. We all enjoyed the cheesecake enormously. And I just thought, "When was the last time these women had so much fun, laughed and laughed at a pure joke. The joke was not on them. No one was put down. It was pure Jesus. A fabulous time for all of us."

A few days later, I went to also celebrate my birthday at Club #1. At this club I knew I needed to let them know at least one day in advance that I was coming. I had a very close relationship with some of the same dancers who were regulars and bartenders. One bartender said, "Dotty, you're always doing stuff for us. We would like to be able to do something for you." So I thought if I don't tell her, she's going to be upset with me. So I let them know a day in advance.

By this time I also become good friends with a male bartender, who had almost become like an adopted son. Oh, my word, Jesus can make such a joyful party out of anything! So my little team and I walked in, and to my surprise there were birthday balloons, presents and a cake for me! (You need to appreciate that some of the cakes that the women get for their birthdays are sexually disgusting.) One of the dancers, knowing I loved to bake for them, was given money by the bartender to buy me gorgeous glass baking pans. This particular dancer met me outside the club several times. She eventually left the club scene, has a successful real estate job, and she found a husband who loves her.

My favorite part of the whole party was a card many of the women had signed. The card said, "You are 70 . . . I don't believe it!" On the inside it said, "I want to see your ID!"

A driving force that keeps me going to the clubs is if the women don't come out, they often go into depression, possible suicide, and are more susceptible to being kidnapped and murdered by serial killers. Plus I know I have a gift from the Lord to do this work.

I would love it if I could pass on the torch and see the Lord raise up other warriors, some to go into the clubs, and others to stand beside them in prayer. My desire is to bring Jesus to these precious souls who are looking for love in all the wrong places. If circumstances would have been different, we all could have ended up in exactly the same places were it not for the grace of God. And my prayer is that many will find the forgiveness of Jesus, and find a whole new life in the Son. But do remember Jesus walked through many dark places, and He loved the unlovely and made them beautiful. He loved women on the streets. He had great compassion on them. He was their forgiver. He did not see them as one bit worse than anyone else. I believe women were his favorites. Maybe I'm a little prejudiced. I don't know. God bless you.

24

CINDERELLA'S SLIPPER

In 2004, Jon and I were going to the Philippines to visit some house churches. We did do that during the mid-section of our three-week journey. However, through a person we met in New Zealand in 1994, we ended up contacting an anti-prostitution ministry in Quezon City, who picked us up at the airport.

The next morning after we arrived, they showed us a documentary describing perfectly how women end up in prostitution. The economy in the Philippines is almost non-existent. Thus, the choices for women amount to working in various kinds of bars (all of which involve prostitution), or trying to eke out a living working in garbage dumps. They have been tricked, sold by parents or guilted into selling themselves, often in order to help support their families. Tragically, however, once they enter the industry they are usually looked down upon by their loved ones, and it becomes almost impossible for them to the exit the dark world they have entered. The most horrific scene in the documentary for me showed the women forced into lesbian activity. This was done to completely humiliate them and break them down so that they would do whatever those who controlled them asked.

After this orientation, we met the highly trained and compassionate staff of this NGO (non-profit) ministry. Then my dream came true and later that evening, we got to go out into the streets with one of the female staff. As we walked along, it was so exciting to see women come out of the dark shadows, like bees to honey, when love walked by in their friend, Tina. Surprisingly, the two Americans with her (us) did not deter them from coming forward and sharing their hearts with Tina. That was the beginning of my love affair with working with women in the sex industry in the Philippines! I felt like Cinderella putting her foot in the magic slipper.

I would stay three or four weeks during my four trips to the Philippines. On my fourth trip in 2010, we went to Angeles City, the second largest sex slavery city, and worked with a different organization. They were amazing. Their focus was on actually going into the clubs. Their strategy was to look for women who were very downcast. You could look at their body language on the stage and see they didn't want to be there, so they could be ripe for hearing about the safe house available to them nearby, which this organization provided.

During our initial trip to the Philippines in January, 2004, we were told about a gathering in May at the Green Lake Conference Center in Wisconsin. The organization that emerged out of that gathering was called ICAP, International Christian Alliance on Prostitution. It was only five hours from our home, so we were able to attend the first conference, and all the subsequent ones. In 2009, ICAP had a regional meeting in Quezon City, Philippines, and we were also privileged to be a part of that. There was an ICAP conference scheduled for November, 2020, but because of Covid it was postponed to November, 2021. It was rescheduled again and came to pass with 150 attendees in November, 2022.

In 2008 I met my precious mentor, Renee Wurzer at ICAP. At ICAP, 2011, she invited me to work with her in the strip clubs in her area, a one and a half hours drive from my home. I was a nervous wreck about doing that, but after thinking about it, I thought about how I had already done this in the Philippines! Then, of course, the trauma of seeing it in your own country close up was appalling. It's like being hit in the face because you did not know this was happening in your very own country, the U.S.A.

For a year and a half I trained with Renee, and the team of volunteers. When she felt I was ready, she gently nudged me out of the nest to start two other strip club ministries in my neck of the woods.

There is a book, *Harrow Sparrow*, by Jill Briscoe, describing a baby bird having to leave the nest and learning to fly that I relate to. I loved working alongside Renee. I was in my comfort zone, very happy and content. I had no plans on leaving my "nest." When Renee handed me a map of Wisconsin, she had circled two clubs closer to my area. With that visual, though terrified, I knew in my heart that the Lord wanted me to spread my wings.

Renee has encouraged me not to go into the clubs too frequently. Because it is a very dark environment, I ask the Lord to nudge me when I'm supposed to go in. My husband and I travel, encouraging home fellowships. In addition to this ministry, if appropriate, I seek to help others to start their own club ministries. And I have seen this happen with women who have very little training, because God is raising new women up to fill the enormous need. It is a pure delight seeing non-judgmental women doing this work here and abroad.

25

BRINGING JESUS INTO THE CLUBS

N ow I will tell you a little bit about what I bring with me into the clubs. I always ask God, "Please show me." I gather things year round, usually from thrift stores. Some people donate items. A precious saint donated some brand new Jesus Calling books, and they are wonderful. I found two beautifully illustrated Easter books. Sometimes I'll find mugs and put iridescent paper in them with teabags as gifts for the women. The see-through paper allows them to view the options, or I may have a piece of jewelry inside the cup. Several other sisters have made beautiful cards and bookmarks for the women.

But I have to tell you about this one fabulous book I found at a thrift store. It looked brand new, and I snatched it up. It was a cookbook called How to Boil Water. I knew one of the women would flip over it! We stopped at one of the clubs I hadn't been to in a long time. Three dancers were there, a sturdy female bouncer who looked the part, and the female bartender. All three dancers had religious backgrounds, which had negative impacts on their upbringing.

I was chatting with one of these women, and I told her that many of the dancers had told me their real names. She said, "I will not tell you my real name." This reveals how often she had been betrayed, which resulted in her extreme woundedness.

When I laid out the books on the bar, which included two Bibles in modern English, my bartender buddy grabbed the How to Boil Water cookbook!

We ended up in a fascinating conversation about her boyfriend. Oh my goodness, that was such a precious night.

Another night at Club #1, there was a bartender who had become a close friend. She could be like a sister to me, but she doesn't know Jesus yet. She told me so many things I needed to hear about two of the women who left their pimps. One of the husbands pimped out his wife. Bless the Lord, she was able to leave him and have custody of her two children.

The other dancer has had many people praying for her for a very long time. When I first met her she was anti-social. As lots of people prayed for her, I saw her change. She became more self-assured, and as a result, I was shocked at what happened. She became very popular as a dancer. I said, "Lord, this is not what we were praying for!" Then when the bartender me that this dancer had left her pimp, I thought, that's what God was doing. It doesn't always look like what we're expecting, but God is at work.

At Club #2 my bartender friend just happened to be in the club that night hanging out. God had her come on that night. I gave her Phillip Yancey's book, What Good is God? and she took it. Oh, my word, how awesome was that! She asked, "Where's your hubby?" And I said, "He's in the car waiting." I could tell she was giving him a star for being a faithful husband and not going into the club. So then she walked out with me and I said, "There's my husband in the car." So she waved to him, oh my word, this is so precious. She walked over to our car, Jon rolled down the window, and she hugged him!

Another monumental thing happened that night. A new dancer was there for her first time, and you could tell she was a sweet young lady. I invited her over to look at the books and the presents. She told me the dancing name she had chosen was "Zoe." I asked, "Do you know what that name means?" She responded, "No." I said, "It means 'life'." She said "Wow. My name means Life!" I had a Jesus Calling book for her. Thank you, Linda, for donating that gift.

Another time when I was at Club #1, there was a woman who came in for an interview dance. Oh, my word, this is America, right? So I was sitting at the bar chatting with the bartender, and had my books and a modern language Bible there. She walked by and she asked, "Is that a Bible?" I said, "Yes, it is, would you like to have it?" She said, "Yes, I would. I have been looking for a Bible." Wow, I thought, can you believe I get to do this?

One time I went to the club on a night when I don't usually visit. A dancer came running up to me when I came in, threw her arms around me and said, "Dotty, I was praying you would come tonight!" Jesus is so amazing that I get such blessings poured over my head.

26

JESUS IS WHOLENESS

I wanted to share this with you. This is a slight adaptation from a page in *Jesus Calling* by Sarah Young:

> Listen to the love song of Jesus. He constantly sings to you. The world's noises are chaotic, having no melody to soothe your soul. But Jesus' voice is so sweet that the birds hush their singing in his presence. Take mini breaks during your days and nights, finding an inner place to be still and listen to Jesus. There is great peace and joy in doing this, taking mental time to seek his face. He loves to reveal himself to you, to speak peace to you, to comfort you, to give you direction for your life. Seek the Lord. He will comfort you with his love. This is the true message of what love is.

In light of this perspective, here's a brief statement from Moving Mountains by John Eldridge. "The search for wholeness compels every person, every hour of their lives, whether they know it or not. We ache to be made whole again, and only one Person, who ever walked this earth can do this for the heart and soul." We seek to encourage wholeness by pointing the women to Jesus Christ.

Jon is very gracious and photocopies some materials for me. I do some artwork to give to the women at the clubs. Some of them have told me they hang them on their walls or mirrors. I usually try to give them a 3 X 5 or some smaller piece of artwork I have painted. I do watercolor, and I will do different paintings, whatever the Lord tells me to do. Sometimes I'll do butterflies, which is such a perfect symbol, going from a caterpillar to a chrysalis to a butterfly. One time I brought in a bird cage, and I put a toy bird in it with the top lifted off. I never tell the women they need to leave. I want to empower them. I let them connect the dots, seeing they're strong enough, and they leave if they are ready to.

Remember, it's dark in these places. If God ever leads you into this type of ministry, you need to be trained, and you need someone to walk through this with you. I'm so thankful the Lord brought Renee into my life to lovingly equip me for a year and a half to bring Jesus into the clubs in the years that were ahead.

27

"WHEN ANY WIFE PRAYS OR PROPHESIES" (1 COR. 11:5)

Because so many women struggle with their "place" in ministry, I am so thankful for my husband. Jon has been a huge help to me in the "Jesus Party" ministry, and he has written a really amazing book called *What's with Paul and Women?* He has done long-term research on the spiritual equality of women with men in the body of Christ, and he addresses the scriptures used to stifle the ministry of women for centuries. He shows how a few verses are misused to suggest women are to be silent in the church. Many church leaders believe Paul was anti-women, but Jon shows that rather he viewed sisters as partners in the gospel, and I think he powerfully proves men and women are one in Christ and totally equal. This perspective has liberated a lot of women, and enabled them to discover more of the mind of Christ regarding sisters.

He has also written *No Will of My Own: How Patriarchy Smothers Female Dignity & Personhood*, another empowering book. He shows from history how women have been marginalized, and basically assigned to be under the feet of men. My grandfather's sexual sins caused far-reaching problems for his wife, his daughters, his son, and me. I had an awesome grandmother who was such a Jesus person to me. I also lived with my Aunt Kay, who was a very angry person. I was her punching bag. Meanwhile my mother was having repeated nervous breakdowns. My mother was put in a mental institution during most of my early childhood. Aunt Kay, seeing what happened to mom in that place, decided she wasn't going to go there, but she was having nervous breakdowns too. She was very hard on me, and truly I had no will of my own. Her words were destructive to me. I felt like I was stupid. The Lord saved me when I was thirteen. You can hear part of my story at Steffa Bene's "The Secret Place" (https://www.youtube.com/watch?v=3o41TcoXlUY).

God bless you in your journey and in whatever your part may be in helping the least of these, those who have no voice. God bless you.

28

"WHEN YOU ENTER THIS PLACE, THE ATMOSPHERE CHANGES"

B efore I leave to visit a club, I send out an email to a number of people who have been praying for me and my team. This way, spiritually I do not go in the Club alone, but I take with me all those who are praying for me and this ministry. When I return home from an evening at a club, I send out a praise report describing how God has answered our prayers. Here is a recent example of what I sent out to my prayer warriors:

Dear precious prayer partners,

I will try to make this short since Jon & I have been out all day & we're pretty exhausted.

It was a very good night! Jesus, along with you all, was before, during & after my visit. I will touch on the highlights. Lots of dancers, not that many customers. All typical at this club.

My dear Jewel, "A," greeted me and accepted the Bible she said she needed & a few other little treasures. A new dancer was there. She showed me a picture of her first child, five months old. She's from Mexico, the father is from Jamaica. I showed her an autobiography of my friend's life in the Philippines. She said she has been to the Philippines! I knew she'd like that book with my friend's story. She is now free from the strip clubs in her country. We talked a long time. She gave me her real estate business card so I could keep in touch with her.

Another new woman was from Thailand. There's no work in her country so she came to the U.S. She can't go back because she refuses to get the shots. She works for a factory in a nearby town & sends $ back to her family, just like many Filipinos do. I saw from her actions that she is so compassionate! She said she cannot read much English but was delighted to take a beautiful Christian children's book. Apparently in Thailand, the only options are Buddhist and Catholic. She appears to be a true Jesus worshipper. What a way to make a living, in a strip club. Although she won't make much at this club, so she might just stay with her factory job, PTL. Both of these women are friends with my Precious "A."

I had some brief, but great conversations with the two Jewels who were beside me when the other dancer full of demons confronted me on my last visit. This time I brought my sword (Bible) and a cool looking sword-looking case. I laid them on the bar & told my bartender friend that I had my Swords with me. Inside the wooden sword-looking case is a jewelry box. LOL.

There was also an older customer who was very curious about what I was doing and happy that I was there for the women.

The manager was there this particular evening. He looked dejected, and said he had a bad headache. Shelley and I asked if we could pray for him. He said, "Yes," and we laid hands on him and lifted him up to the Lord. Out of the blue, he then announced, "When you come into this place, the atmosphere in here changes." Wow!

We hit a small deer on the way home but the Lord and your prayers totally protected us! Only a few hairs from the deer were visible on the bumper! Thank you Jesus, thank you prayer partners, and our well-built 2007 Volvo!

Please pray that what was given out tonight, including home-made cards, verses & Jesus stories will penetrate their hearts with Jesus's Love for them.

Blessings on all of you, Dotty (August, 2022)

TWO STEPS FORWARD, ONE STEP BACKWARDS

W ell, tying up this book is a bit of a challenge. There's so much I want to say, and so many stories that have not been included. Some of them very exciting, and others also exciting but not in a good way.

I think I mentioned that when Jon and I were in the Philippines and went out on the streets, we ministered to the street women, as opposed to women who worked in bars. I felt like I put my foot in Cinderella's shoe! All the many missionary trips I've made beforehand, including the nine trips to Romania, several to Haiti, etc., were in preparation for this newly-found ministry. Shockingly, I had no idea at that time what the young women in the Romanian orphanages had been through. I had no idea of the sexual exploitation that they had to endure in order to survive in such places.

Although very happy with what the Lord has given me to do, I do not want you to think there aren't extreme sorrows in this work. Women disappear and I do not know what happened to them. Have they been moved by a pimp on the run, which I think is common, or have they gotten into a customer's car or met him or her at a motel, and then been maimed or murdered . . . a faceless non-person to them, who just used and then disposed of them.

The reality is some of these women are believers in Christ, women who have had such horrific backgrounds that they were either sold or guilt was used to force them into doing that work, or they were made to feel like that's all they were worth, so their thinking is that they might as well just live up to what's expected of them. Too many have disappeared from my life, and I have had no further contact with them.

But there are also beautiful success stories of some who have left. So I end with this . . . I messaged one of the Jewels that Jon and I both visited outside the club. It was Christmas a few years ago, and our family was not celebrating on that day. I texted one of the women I have known for quite some time and asked her if she had food. She texted me that she did not, so I quickly rounded up some food and took it over to her. We found out it wasn't so much about her, but her roommate, "V." I barely had a conversation with "V" at the club, but she remembered me and my name. We sat there with her for hours and had a beautiful, beautiful time. She said her mother had told her all of her life that she was crazy. Actually, it was the mother who was crazy. But when "V" heard it enough times, she could cave in to the lie.

Another time shortly after that she asked us if we would like to come over and have a Bible study with her! Of course, we grabbed our goodies and hopped over there! We had a precious time with her. We are not religious, we are Jesus lovers. She said it was the best Sunday she has ever had in her life! It was fantastic for us too. At that time "The Shack" movie was playing in a theater near her. It was kind of an interesting time in that movie theater, because she's on medication, and she was drinking caffeine like crazy, and smoking. She was restless, in and out of her seat, not like your typical movie experience . . . lol. Of course she didn't catch the whole theme of the movie, but I think she really enjoyed it. And she enjoyed our time together.

Weeks later I checked in to see how she was doing. Let me tell you, it was awesome. She said, "Oh Dotty, I need all of Jon's books. All of them. I lost them in my move," but she said, "I still have the Bible you gave me." We were both so excited! She kept her Bible in modern English that I had given her. We gathered presents for "V," including a Bible adult coloring book, maple syrup, a mug, scarf, the Jesus Calling book, a journaling book on writing your story, and the book, The Unselfishness of God, by Hannah Whitehall Smith, and several other treasures, all inside a large Easter basket. Perfect, since it was close to Easter. Leave it to Jesus for the timing! Her last page is not written yet either.

Thank you all! I pray God will use this book, simple though it is, in all its informality. May the Lord use it for God's glory and to spread the word to those who have been shut away in shame. Before I was made aware, I did not know who these Precious Jewels were and why they are there.

May God bless you.

REFERENCES

For further reading: Nita Belles, *In Our Backyard: A Christian Perspective on Human Trafficking in the United States*, Free River, 2011, 175 pp.

ABOUT THE AUTHOR AND EDITOR

Dotty Zens was born in Teaneck, New Jersey. After high school she went off to a Bible college in the South for three and a half years, with interests in art and missions. Her first mission trip was to Mexico in 1966, and then to India in 1967. She met Jon in September, 1967, and they were married in June, 1968, intending to go to northeast India to work in an orphanage. Since 1992, she has made nine trips to Romania (four with Jon), four trips to the Philippines (two with Jon), three trips to Haiti, and trips to Moldova and China. In 2004 her work with those in the sex trade began in the Philippines. Since 2011 she has been ministering in American strip clubs, mostly in Wisconsin. She raised three children, and has six grandchildren, and one great grandchild. She loves face painting in various settings, organic gardening, and baking from scratch.

Five days after Dotty was born in NJ, Jon Zens was born in Barstow, California. After two years as an art major at CalState/Northridge, he left for the same Bible college Dotty was attending. Jon then transferred to Covenant College and finished a B.A. in Biblical Studies. When their visa to India was turned down, Jon continued studies at Westminster Seminary in Philadelphia and completed an M.Div. in 1972. After moving to Nashville in 1975, Jon became the editor of *Baptist Reformation Review* in 1978. The name of the quarterly was changed to Searching Together in 1982, and he has continued as editor for forty-five years. In 1983 he received a D.Min. from the California Graduate School of Theology. His recent books include *Jesus Is Family: His Life Together, Elusive Community: Why Do We Avoid What*

We Were Created For? and *We Are Christ on Earth: The Visible Expression of Jesus in Space and Time.*

For more information about Dotty Zens,
or to contact her, please write to:
Dotty Zens
PO Box 548
St. Croix Falls, WI 54024
715-338-4261; jzens@searchingtogether.org

Many Voices. One Message

www.quoir.com

CPSIA information can be obtained
at www.ICGtesting.com
Printed in the USA
JSHW012034190323
39091JS00004B/6